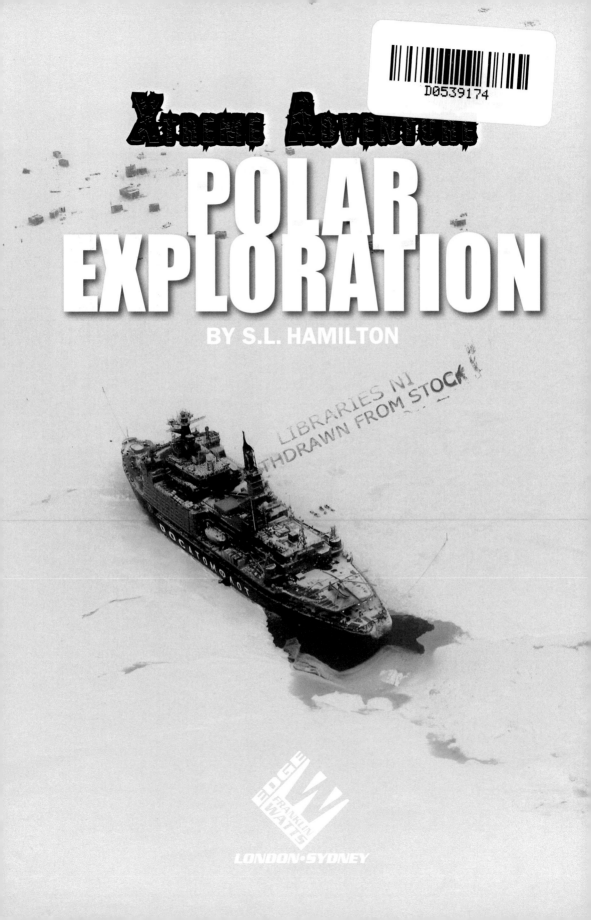

Xtreme Adventure
POLAR EXPLORATION

BY S.L. HAMILTON

EDGE
FRANKLIN WATTS
LONDON•SYDNEY

Franklin Watts
First published in Great Britain in 2015 by The Watts Publishing Group

First published in the USA by ABDO Publishing Company.

Editor: John Hamilton
Graphic Design: Sue Hamilton
Cover Design: Sue Hamilton

Acknowledgements:
Cover Photo: Corbis
Interior Photos: AP-pgs 6-7, 12, 15, 30-31, 32; Corbis-pgs 22-23 & 29; Getty-pgs 4-5,
8-9, 10-11, 14, 18 (left), 19 (left middle and bottom), 21 & 28; iStock-pg 18 (right top);
NASA-pgs 2-3; National Geographic-pgs 13 & 24-25; NOAA-pgs 20 & 26; Thinkstock-pgs
7 (inset), 9 (inset), 18 (right bottom), 19 (left top, right top & right bottom) , 27, 30
(inset) & 31 (inset); U.S. Coast Guard-pg 1; U.S. Navy-pgs 16-17.

Every attempt has been made to clear copyright. Should there be any inadvertent
omission please apply to the publisher for rectification.

Dewey number 910.9'11
HB ISBN 978 1 4451 4078 0
Library ebook ISBN 978 1 4451 4079 7

Printed in China

Franklin Watts
An imprint of
Hachette Children's Group
Part of The Watts Publishing Group
Carmelite House
50 Victoria Embankment
London EC4Y 0DZ

An Hachette UK Company
www.hachette.co.uk

www.franklinwatts.co.uk

CONTENTS

POLAR EXPLORATION

The North and South Poles are two of the harshest environments on Earth. Temperatures never rise above freezing at the South Pole. The North Pole may reach 0 degrees Celsius on a 'hot' summer day. Still, scientists, explorers and adventurers are drawn to these icy realms.

КАПИТАН ХЛЕБНИКОВ

QUARK EXPEDITIONS

XTREME QUOTE – *"We on this journey were already beginning to think of death as a friend."*
– Apsley Cherry-Garrard, Antarctic Explorer 1910–1913

The first humans reached the North* and South Poles a little over 100 years ago. Modern transportation and equipment have made it easier for people to reach these frozen wastelands. Yet adventurers must carry all the supplies they need to survive. The poles are mostly unexplored. Brave explorers get to see what few people have seen before.

Tourists from the icebreaker ship Kapitan Khlebnikov begin an ice hike in Antarctica.

*People can't agree on when this actually happened.

GETTING TO THE POLES

Early explorers to the poles travelled by ship as far as they could. Then they crossed the snowy landscapes by walking, skiing or using dogsleds.

XTREME FACT– Neither the North Pole nor the South Pole are owned by any one nation.

Today, getting to the poles is simpler, but expensive. People travel by ship or plane. Visitors head to the North Pole in the northern hemisphere's summer

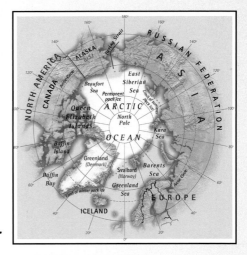

months. Ships called icebreakers cut their way through the Arctic ice. They depart from Alaska, Norway and Russia. Some adventurers fly to the North Pole. Planes and helicopters land on the ice. People can walk or ski the final distance to precisely 90 degrees north latitude.

An icebreaker ship takes a group of adventurers to the North Pole.

Travelling to the South Pole is more difficult. Cruise ships leave from Australia, New Zealand, Argentina and Chile, and sail to the frozen continent of Antarctica. Some trips take passengers very far south, but others only take people to the Antarctic Peninsula and Southern Ocean islands. There are also ski plane flights that bring visitors right to the South Pole.

Since the South
Pole is really
only occupied by
scientists, there
are not many
places to stay.
Tent camps are
set up during the
Antarctic summer,
from November to January.

POLAR GEAR

Even during summer, the poles are bitterly cold, usually below freezing. Adventurers must have parkas, snowsuits, mittens, balaclavas, scarves, warm socks and boots.

Skis and ski poles, water bottles, rope and backpacks with emergency tents and first-aid kits are important for those setting out to explore. A pair of goggles or sunglasses is also important. During each polar region's summer, the sun does not set. The brilliant sunshine can be blinding.

Polar explorers often use pulks (below) to carry their supplies. These small, runnerless sleds glide across deep snow. They are designed to carry a lot of gear in a small space. Items are secured into place using straps. A waterproof cover sits on top.

The lightweight pulk's harness attaches to a person or an animal, such as a dog or reindeer. Pulks are designed to easily manoeuvre across steep or rough terrain.

XTREME FACT – A larger pulk sled is called an ahkio [ah-kee-oh].

DANGERS

The greatest danger at the poles is the bitter cold. Strong blowing winds can cause 'whiteouts', making it impossible to see what's ahead. It is easy to get lost or disorientated even when just a few steps away from camp.

Polar bears are a danger to humans travelling to the North Pole. These powerful bears weigh anywhere from 150—544 kg. Polar bears have a good sense of smell. They only live in the Arctic and do not hibernate. They prefer to eat seals, but will attack and eat humans.

XTREME FACT – It's possible to get frostbite and sunburn at the same time at the poles.

North Pole Adventures

Adventurers to the North Pole may see a 'pole', but it does not mark the actual North Pole. This is because the Arctic is really just a huge series of ice sheets sitting on top of the ocean. The ice sheets move all the time. A person can set down a pole, but by the next day, it will have moved.

XTREME FACT – The North Pole has one sunrise (at the March equinox) and one sunset (at the September equinox). The sun stays above the horizon in the summer, and below the horizon in the winter.

The crew of the United States submarine USS Hampton posts a sign reading 'North Pole' after surfacing in the polar ice cap region.

Many land mammals live in the Arctic polar region because it is surrounded by land. Adventurers may see animals, such as musk oxen, reindeer, caribou, foxes, hares, wolves, lemmings and polar bears. (Polar bears are often considered marine mammals because they live most of their lives on the polar ice pack.)

Musk Ox

Reindeer

Caribou

Arctic Fox

Wolf

Lemming

Polar Bear

Arctic Hare

The North Pole's surrounding Arctic waters are filled with marine mammals. Whales, porpoises, seals and walruses may be seen by Arctic visitors. These species capture their prey in the Arctic Ocean. All of these animals are also sometimes hunted by people living in the Arctic region.

Walrus

XTREME FACT – There aren't any penguins in the Arctic.

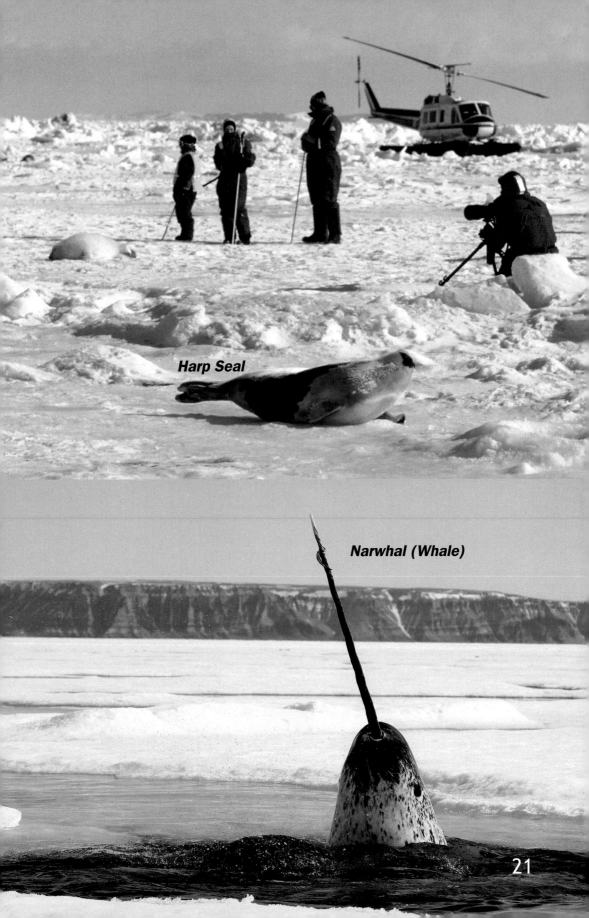

Harp Seal

Narwhal (Whale)

21

SOUTH POLE ADVENTURES

Adventurers come to Antarctica by ship and by plane. After making their way to the southernmost point of the continent, they can touch an actual pole that is called the 'ceremonial' South Pole.

XTREME FACT – Scientists working in Antarctica call the continent 'The Ice'. It is the coldest place on Earth. The South Pole never gets temperatures above freezing.

The cermonial South Pole stands near the Amundsen-Scott South Pole Station. The station is a scientific research base funded by the United States.

Ceremonial South Pole Marker

The 'geographic' South Pole is a stationary point on the ground. It is where all the lines of longitude come together at 90 degrees south latitude. This location has to be marked each year. The thick ice sheet that covers the land at the South Pole moves about 9 metres each year, taking the marker with it.

GEOGRAPHIC
SOUTH
POLE

ROALD AMUNDSEN
DECEMBER 14, 1911

"So we arrived and were able to plant our flag at the geographical South Pole."

ROBERT F. SCO*
JANUARY 17, 1912

"The Pole. Yes, but under very different circumstances from those expected."

ELEVATION 9,301 FT.

XTREME FACT – Norwegian Roald Amundsen and his party were the first people to reach the South Pole on 14 December, 1911.

Geographic South Pole Marker

Antarctica is as big as the United States and Mexico combined. However, there are no permanent residents. Every visitor stays for a period of time then leaves.

A marine scientist poses with killer whales swimming in the Ross Sea, Antarctica.

Very few creatures live near the South Pole. The largest is an insect, a 1 millimetre midge. Marine mammals such as whales, porpoises and seals, and birds such as penguins, live near the coastal regions of Antarctica.

Midge

Gentoo
Penguins

XTREME FACT – There aren't any polar bears in Antarctica.

SEA ICE

There are many different kinds of ice formation at the poles. The North Pole sits on thick sheets of ice over the Arctic Ocean. These big ice floes bump into each other, creating piles of tall ridges.

A polar explorer climbs over a pressure ridge made of sea ice on her way to the North Pole.

The South Pole is on the continent of Antarctica. This land mass is surrounded by sea ice. Adventurers arriving by boat view sea ice floating in the surrounding ocean waters. Some ice eventually floats northward and melts.

A ship on its way to Antarctica is surrounded by sea ice.

GLOSSARY

AMUNDSEN-SCOTT SOUTH POLE STATION
A scientific research station located at the southernmost place on Earth, the geographic South Pole. It is funded by the US National Science Foundation.

Balaclava

BALACLAVA
A cap-like piece of clothing that clings tightly to the head and neck, leaving only the eyes, and sometimes the mouth, exposed.

CONTINENT
One of the seven main landmasses that make up the Earth's land surface.

EQUINOX
Two days during the year, usually 20 March and 22 September, when the Earth's orbit and the tilt of its axis causes the sun's rays to shine directly on the equator.

FROSTBITE
Damage to skin caused by severe cold.

HIBERNATE
When a warm-blooded animal goes into an extended sleep for the winter. Black bears hibernate, but polar bears do not.

HEMISPHERE
Half of the Earth, divided into northern and southern halves by the equator.

ICE FLOE
A sheet of ice floating on the surface of the water.

ICEBREAKER
A type of tough ship built to break surface ice and allow the vessel to pass through the water undamaged.

LATITUDE AND LONGITUDE
A grid system marked in degrees that is used to pinpoint any place on the surface of the Earth. The east-west lines are latitude. The north-south lines are longitude.

SEA ICE
Frozen seawater. Much of the Earth's sea ice is located around the planet's poles.

WHITEOUT
When heavy snow and wind combine to make it impossible for a person to see what is around them.

INDEX